Jesus Heals

by Akram Zaki

Illustrated by Paulo Gaviola

a true story about JESUS

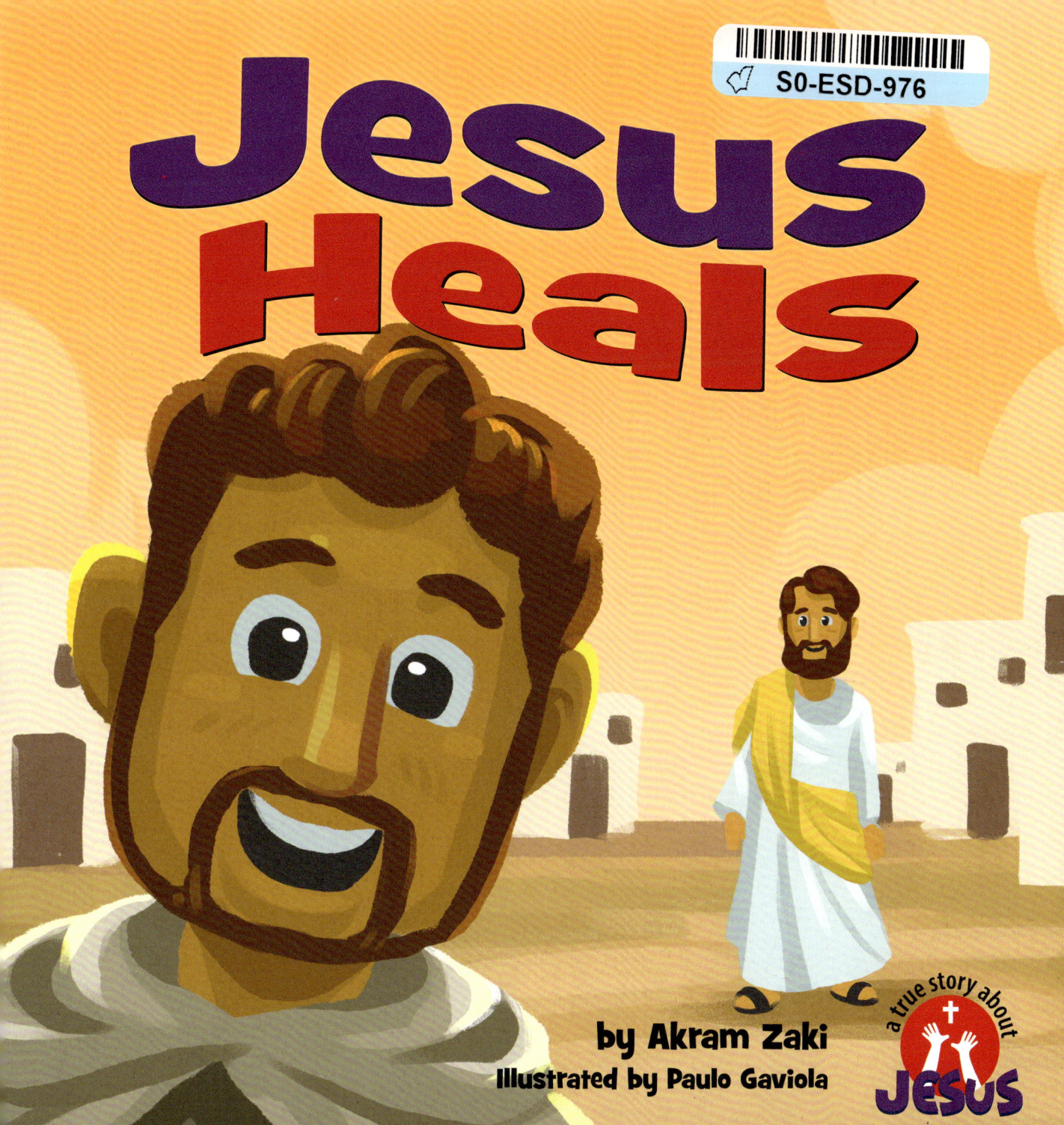

First Printing: August 2023

Copyright © 2023 by Akram Zaki. All rights reserved. No part of this book may be reproduced, copied, broadcast, stored, or shared in any form whatsoever without written permission from the publisher, except in the case of brief quotations in articles and reviews. For more information write: Master Books, PO Box 726, Green Forest, AR 72638

Master Books® is a division of the New Leaf Publishing Group, LLC.

Please consider requesting that a copy of this volume be purchased by your local library system.

ISBN-13: 978-1-68344-339-1
ISBN-13: 978-1-61458-840-5 (digital)
Library of Congress: 2023930814
Printed in China

Scripture quotations marked (NIV) are taken from the Holy Bible, New International Version®, NIV®. Copyright © 1973, 1978, 1984, 2011 by Biblica, Inc.™ Used by permission of Zondervan. All rights reserved worldwide.

Please visit our website for other great titles:
www.masterbooks.com

For information regarding promotional opportunities, please contact the publicity department at pr@nlpg.com.

Master Books®
A Division of New Leaf Publishing Group
www.masterbooks.com

This is a true story about Jesus. It comes from Matthew Chapter 8 in your Bible.

One day Jesus was walking with His disciples when a man with leprosy met him on the road.

(Leprosy is a terrible skin disease.)

The man was lonely, he was sick, and he was afraid. The people around him called him unclean.

The man's doctors couldn't help him, and no one the man knew was willing to be near him anymore. They would all run away when they saw him coming, or throw rocks at him until he went away. They were afraid they would get leprosy too.

He couldn't even go to the temple to give God a gift or to pray, because lepers weren't allowed there.

Jesus didn't run away,
and He didn't tell him to
go away,
either.

Jesus didn't even frown when He smelled the man's dirty clothes and sick skin.

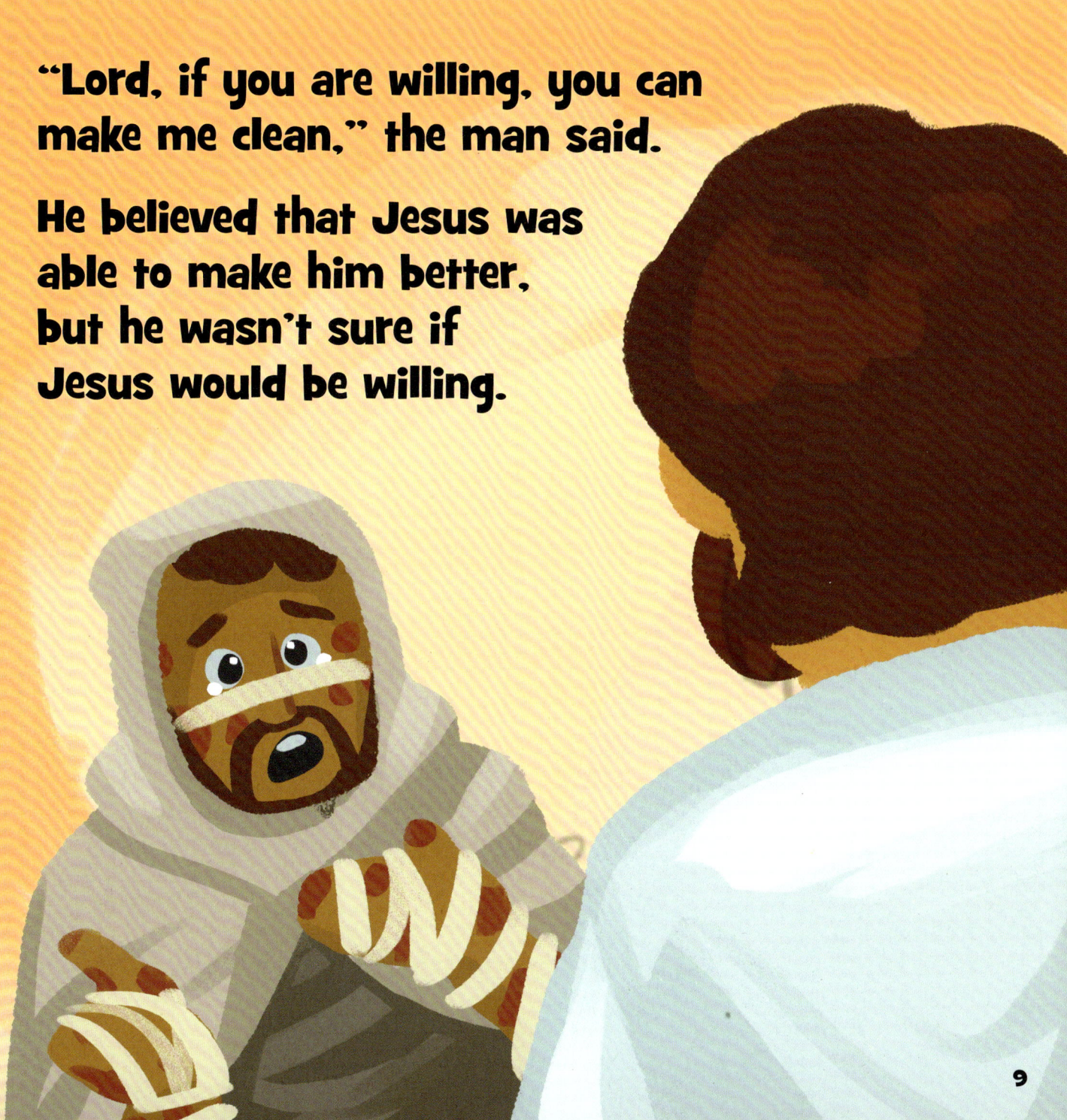

"Lord, if you are willing, you can make me clean," the man said.

He believed that Jesus was able to make him better, but he wasn't sure if Jesus would be willing.

Jesus smiled. Then He did something that no one had done for a very long time.

He reached out His hand and touched the man.

The man had missed being touched, being hugged, and being loved. He missed his wife and his friends, he missed going to the temple, and he missed his home. His body was sore and it hurt all over. He was tired, lonely, and sad.

For so long the man had been too sick to be loved. No one had wanted to be near him.

But not Jesus.

Suddenly the man felt different. He looked at his hands and arms. They looked different. He couldn't feel the pain of his sores anymore. His sores and spots were gone!

The man laughed in excitement and looked down at his feet and legs. He felt his face and his ears. They felt normal again!

The leprosy was gone!

"Go to the temple and give God a gift," said Jesus.

"You are most welcome there."

The man went to the temple to thank God for what Jesus had done for him.

Then he returned home to see his family and friends.

He had missed them so much, and thanks to Jesus, he could be with them again.

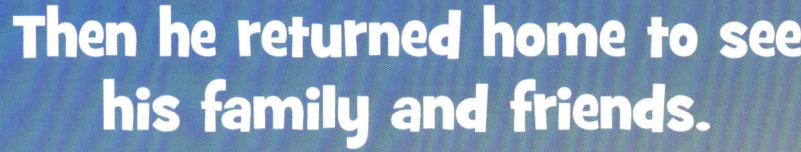

Jesus loved and accepted the man even before he was cured.

No one else would do that.

He healed the man, and He even gave the man the ability to give a gift to God.

No one else could do that.

Jesus is always willing to help us when we call out to Him.

There is no one else like
JESUS.

Heal me, Lord, and I will be healed;
save me and I will be saved, for you
are the one I praise.

Jeremiah 17:14 (NIV)

You can read this true story in the Bible. This story was written down by a man called Matthew, one of Jesus' disciples (followers).

Matthew saw and heard many things that Jesus did and said. He wrote them down for us so we could learn about how wonderful Jesus is.

You can find his stories about Jesus in the Bible in the Gospel of Matthew.